# CRAZED WOMEN

## (THE BAKKHAI)

*Euripides*

*translated by
Laurence Senelick*

**BROADWAY PLAY PUBLISHING INC**
New York
www.broadwayplaypublishing.com
info@broadwayplaypublishing.com

CRAZED WOMEN
© Copyright 2014 by Laurence Senelick

First printing: December 2014
I S B N: 978-0-88145-624-0
Book design: Marie Donovan
Page make-up: Adobe Indesign
Typeface: Palatino

Of the hundred or so plays Euripides wrote in his lifetime only nineteen survive. Not all of them won first prize at the festivals, but BAKKHAI, produced in 405 B C E, soon after its author's death, did. It was still well enough known in the fourth century C E, at least as a text, that Gregory Nazianzos, bishop of Constantinople, lifted many of its lines for his dramatic trilogy, *The Passion of Christ*. Speeches of Dionysos, Agaue and others were put in the mouths of Christ, the Virgin Mary and the Beloved Disciple John. His version also preserves lines missing at the denouement of Euripides' play in extant manuscripts. Although highly esteemed by Goethe, BAKKHAI owes its modern resurrection to fin de siècle aesthetes, who promoted the notion of Euripides as a sensitive and humane soul. The play had another resurgence in the Psychedelic Psixties with Dionysos presented as a pot-smoking Flower Child and Pentheus as a representative of the military industrial complex.

BAKKHAI holds an irresistible fascination for an era befuddled by Nietzsche's "God is dead" and appalled by its own savagery. Untamed passion and the intrusion of an irrational divinity into our well-conducted civilization need to be explained. Subjected to every religious interpretation, the eternal recurrence of the resurrection myth of Dionysos and the dismembered and then reassembled Pentheus could be made to configure the tragic disruptions that interrupt life's impulses to higher things. Euripides never rationalizes or justifies, however. Instead, he presents us the contradictions and leaves it to us to make sense of them.

*Laurence Senelick*

# CHARACTERS

DIONYSOS
TEIRESIAS
KADMOS
PENTHEUS
GUARD
FIRST MESSENGER (*herdsman*)
SECOND MESSENGER (*house slave*)
AGAUE
CHORUS *of Asian Women*

# PROLOGUE

DIONYSOS

Joy to the world, the Lord is come!
The son of God,
I, me, myself, Dionysos,
In the land of Thebes, back where I was born,
Fathered by Zeus on the eldest daughter of King Kadmos,
Semele; delivered by a flash of lightning, not a midwife.
My looks are not god-like, for I have morphed to mortal
    flesh
To pay this visit to my native parts,
By Dirké's stream and the waters of Ismenos.
Look, there stands the tomb of my literally thunder-struck
    mother,
Close beside the ruins of the house she lived in,—tread softly
    here—
Still smoking, smoldering, zapped by the living spark of
    Zeus's flame,
A souvenir of his wife Hera's undying hatred for my mother.
Three cheers for Kadmos, who sanctified this spot,
A shrine to his daughter, and three cheers for me who
    nestled it
Among the leaves of clustering vines.
I did it after I had left the rich gold-fields of Lydia
And Phrygia, the sun-burnt flatlands of Persia, the
Walled towns of Bactria and the bleak country of
The Medes, crossing prosperous Arabia
And all of Asia that lies along the salty sea waters
Where Greeks and barbarians live cheek by jowl
In their cities gorgeous with towers.
Now that I have established my secret rites there
And set their people dancing, so that those mortals grant my

Status as a god, I have come to this Greek city.
Thebes first, before any other city in Greece,—
Here I inspired the women to whoop and holler and drape
    their bodies
With fawnskins, here I put in their hands my throbbing
    shaft,
The ivy-entwined joyrod.
Thebes first, because my mothers' sisters, who of all people
should know better,
Said that I, Dionysos, was not the seed of Zeus,
But rather that Semele had been seduced by some mortal,
And, at the cunning suggestion of her father Kadmos, laid
    the shameful
Loss of her virginity on Zeus. "For lying about the man she
    fucked
The god blasted her with lightning."
This story her gloating sisters put in circulation, which is
    why
I worked those sisters up to a frenzy, drove them from home
To live mindless in the mountains, spurred them to
Wear the uniform of my religion.
Whatever women were of Kadmos's blood
I drove crazed from their houses,
And now along with Kadmos's daughters they sit
Beneath the green pines on roofless rocks.
For this city, still unacquainted with my rites,
The rites of Bakkhos,
Must learn this lesson to the bitter end,
Kicking and screaming if that's the way they want it,
And my mother Semele's reputation will be restored
When I prove to mortals that I am indeed the son of God.

Now it so happens that old Kadmos turned his kingship
Over to my cousin Pentheus,
Who wages war on the gods, me in particular, excluding me
    from
The wine offerings and leaving my name out of official
    prayers.
So I intend to teach him an object lesson in my divinity,
Him and all his Thebans. And then, my work being done
    here,

I'll turn my attention to some other city, and treat them to an
   epiphany of me.
But if the Thebans try by force of arms to drive my followers,
The Bakkhai, from the mountains, I shall lead my maddened
   women into battle.
One more reason for sloughing off my divine form and
   morphing into human shape.
Now let the games begin!
O ye who have left the Tmolian hills that ring round Lydia,
My adoring sorority, women of Asia, bosom companions of
Mine in fun and festivities,
Come and beat the Phrygian tomtoms
Which I invented, me and earth-mother Rhea;
Beat out your rhythm before the house of King
Pentheus, so that the city of Kadmos can feast its eyes on
   you.
Meanwhile I'm off to join the Bakkhai in the thickets
Of Mount Kithairon, and kick up my heels.

## PARODOS

### CHORUS

From the land of Asia
Swooping down from holy Tmolos here I come,
Swift to do the sweet bidding of
Bellowing Bromios
(Hard labor that rests and refreshes me),
To cry "Euoi," all hail Lord Bakkhos.
Who is on the roads? Who?
Who is in the palace? Who?
Let him emerge from the darkness, let tongues hush in
   reverence,
Shun all things ill-omened;
For I shall sing now and forever the old-time hymns
To Dionysos.
O,
Blessèd the one, happy and fortunate,
Who knows what is sacred to the gods,
Leads a life of pious service and is imbued

In his innermost soul with their mysteries;
Blessèd the one who, celebrating the Bakkhai's holy revels
In the mountains
And the lofty orgies of Great Mother Kybele,
Waving up and down the mystic joyrod,
His head crowned with ivy, serves
Dionysos.

Come, Bakkhai, come, Bakkhai,
Escort the god and son of god,
Dionysos!
Bring him from the Phrygian mountains
To Greece's spacious streets, wide enough to dance in,
Bring home Bellowing Bromios!
Once upon a time his pregnant mother
Went into labor all untimely,
Prompted by Zeus's urgent lightning,
And from her belly, heaving,
Cast forth the preemie,
His life cancelling out hers.
In the birthing room Zeus son of Time
Instantly caught up the babe
And concealed him within his thigh

Suturing the wound with golden pins,
To keep him hidden from his consort Hera.

And in the fullness of time, God gave birth to the
Bull-horned god,
And crowned him with a crown of snakes,
Which is why his followers interweave
That brood of cattle-killers in their hair.

O nurse of Semele, Thebes,
Crown your head with ivy;
Burgeon, burgeon with dense foliage
Of holly-berried bryony,
And consecrate yourselves with twigs of oak
Or evergreen,
And trim your garments, well dappled fawnskins,
With white-haired tufts
Of wool. Take the thrusting joyrods of fennel
And purify them. Now, right now the people of this land
  must

Dance—for the lord of the dance is Bellowing Bromios
Who leads his throngs of revellers
To the mountain, to the mountain where
The mob of women waits,
Goaded from their looms, stung from their spinning by
Dionysos.

O
Secret chambers of the sylvan youths,
The holiest hollows of Crete,
A shelter for the birth of Dionysos,
Where in the cave triple-crested
My male devotees, priestly eunuchs, effeminate youths,
Found me and were the first whose
Feet whirled in frenzy to the beat of
The taut leather tomtom,
Mingling it with the sweet squeal of
The Phrygian pipes, and later put it
In the hands of Earth-mother Rhea
To accompany the ecstatic cries
Of her worshipping women.
Stolen from her by the lawless satyrs,
Goat-men with pricks erect, now the drum
Beats time to the dance
At the festival which every second year
Celebrates your name
Dionysos!
Welcome and well-favored is he in the mountains he comes
    from.
When he drops to the ground, run down by the packs in full
    cry,
When he puts on the sacred fawn-skin.
When he hunts the wild goat and sheds its blood.
When he revels in gnawing its raw, living flesh.
When he runs to the mountains of Phrygia, runs to the
mountains of Lydia!
He is our leader, he is Bellowing Bromios!
Euoi!

With white milk the earth runs! With red wine the earth
   runs!
It runs with the nectar of bees.

God of the Bakkhai, brandishing the blazing pine torch,
Aromatic as the smoke of Syrian frankincense,
Trailing the flames from his joyrod,
Running and dancing,
Stirring up the stragglers and
Spurring them on with his cries,
Driving them back to the dance-line,
Tossing his long lovelocks in the breeze!

Amidst the Maenads' cries his voice rings deep, Euoi!
On, on, my Bakkhai!
On, on, my Bakkhai!
You glory of gold-streaked Tmolos,
Sing the praises of Dionysos
To the beat of the booming drum,
Exalting in ecstasy the master of ecstasy
Amidst the Phrygian shrilling and shouting,
When the sacred mellifluous flute
Pipes the sacred song of sacred mirth,
Climbing with you as you climb—
To the mountain! To the mountain!

In true ecstasy then, like a foal in a pasture beside its mother
   grazing,
With taut limbs and fleet feet the Bacchant leaps!


## FIRST EPISODE

Who's on guard duty? Call from the house Kadmos
Son of Agenor, the man who left the city of Sidon and
Built the towers of this city of Thebes.
Go, someone, let him know that Teiresias
Is waiting for him; he knows full well the reason I've
Come here, agreeable to the pact we made, one old man
With an older one, to concoct joyrods and wear
Fawn-skins and crown our heads with ivy wreaths.

KADMOS

My good old friend, I heard your voice while still in the
  house
And recognized in it a wise man's wisdom.
Look, here I am already suited up in the god's team colors;
Which is only right, considering he is my daughter's son,
Dionysos who reveals himself a god to man.
His greatness must be honored to the fullest extent.
Where do I go to do my dancing, where are we to stamp our
  feet
And shake our gray heads? Spell it out for me,
One geezer to another, Teiresias; for you're the wise one.
I don't think I'll ever weary night and day of
Thwacking my joyrod on the ground; it is sweet to forget
How old we are.

TEIRESIAS

I know just how you feel
For I too shall kick up my heels like a teenage boy.

KADMOS

Would it be all right if we took a chariot as far as the
mountain?

TEIRESIAS

No, for that might seem disrespectful to the god.

KADMOS

Is an old man like me supposed to lead you, another old
  man, like a toddler?

TEIRESIAS

The god will see to it we'll have no trouble getting there.

KADMOS

Say, are we the only free males in the city to dance for
  Bakkhos?

TEIRESIAS

Yes, for we're the only ones who know what we're doing.
The rest are fools.

KADMOS

Enough dawdling. Come, take my hand.

TEIRESIAS

There, grasp my hand and make a pair of them.

KADMOS

I may be just a mortal, but you won't find me neglecting the
gods.

TEIRESIAS

But let's not try to second-guess them either.
The traditions handed down by our ancestors
From time immemorial cannot be wrestled to the mat by
Logic, no matter how clever agnostics may think they are.

KADMOS

Suppose somebody says: aren't you ashamed at your age
To go dancing with ivy on your head?

TEIRESIAS

Never you mind. The god didn't say that dancing
Is exclusively for the young or, for that matter, the old.
He wishes to be honored by everyone
In common, to be the chosen one though not to share his
    honors.

KADMOS

Since your eyes cannot see the light, Teiresias
I shall interpret for you by means of words.
Here comes Pentheus to the house in haste,
The son of Echion, to whom I handed over power in the
    land;
What a state he's in! What on earth is he going to say?

PENTHEUS

The minute I go out of town
I hear of some new brand of evil befalling the city,
Of our women leaving home
To plunge into bogus revels and gad about
Shady mountains, dancing in honor of

The latest thing in gods, Dionysos,
Whoever he is;
Drinking from brimming punch-bowls,
Slinking off one by one to isolated hideaways
To gratify the lusts of men,
Pretending they're maenads, priestesses engaged in sacred
    intercourse,
But worshipping the goddess of hot sex more than the god
    of wine.
Those I could capture are safely guarded
Hands cuffed, under lock and key in the common jail;
Those still at large I shall hunt from the mountain,
And to name names, Aktaion's mother, Antonoë,
My aunt Ino and even Agaue, the mother who bore me to
    Echion.
I shall clap them in irons
And put a quick end to this Bacchic trickery.
And now I hear some foreigner has turned up,
A spell-binding con-man come to our native land from
    Lydia,
With golden ringlets of perfumed hair,
His cheeks flushed with wine, and the allure of lust in his
    eyes,
Who day and night chats up the girls,
Dangling before them his pleasure-giving paraphernalia.
If I ever get him inside these walls
I'll soon stop him thwacking his joyrod and tossing
The hair from his eyes. How? Simple: by cleaving his head
    from his body.
So this man claims Dionysos is a god, eh?
So this man says the god was once sewn into Zeus's thigh?
The fact of the matter is Dionysos was struck by lightning
Along with his mother, because she lied and said she'd had
    sex with Zeus.
Lies like that are an abomination, one that calls for hanging
    by the neck,
Aren't they outrageous, whoever this Stranger is supposed
    to be?
Will wonders never cease! Here's the prophet
Teiresias tricked out in fashionable fawnskins

And my mother's father—I have to laugh!—
Bacchanting around with a joyrod. Sir, it turns my stomach
To see someone as old as you act so absurdly.
Won't you shake off the ivy? Won't you come to your senses
And drop the joyrod, granddad?
This is all your fault, Teiresias; you have to have another
God. By introducing this one to mankind as a novelty
You expect to make fresh profits off your bird-watching,
To take more money for decoding the signs in burnt
    offerings, don't you?
If you weren't senile and decrepit,
I'd toss your ass in jail along with those crazy Bakkhai,
For popularizing such obscene initiation rites. For when
    women
At their banquets indulge in the joys of the lustrous grape,
The party is bound to come to a bad end. That's what I think!

CHORUS

Blasphemy! You strange man, do you not respect the gods
And Kadmos who sowed the dragon's seed?
Will you the son of Echion disgrace his clan?

TEIRESIAS

When an intelligent man makes a strong argument the
Basis for his speech, it's no wonder his speech is eloquent.
But your tongue runs more smoothly than your brains,
And there are no thoughts behind your words.
Any man who speaks so glibly and complacently and
Without an ounce of sense puts the whole community at
    risk.
This new god, the one you ridicule,
I'm at a loss for words to express how very great
He shall be all over Greece.
For, young man, there are two primal elements
In human life: one, the goddess Demeter
Who is Earth,—call her by whatever name you please;—
She nourishes mortals with solid food;
Then he came, the child of Semele. To partner Demeter
He discovered the liquor of the grape and brought it
To mortals. He gives surcease to men's long-suffering
Sorrows when they are filled with the distillation of the vine,

And he brings sleep that "knits up the ravell'd sleave of
    care,"
Sleep that is "sore labour's bath, balm of hurt minds."
He, himself a god, is poured out as an offering to the other
    gods,
Which is how mortals here below praise god from whom all
    blessings flow.
And you laugh at him for having been sewn into Zeus's
Thigh? Let me explain what a clever metaphor that is.
When Zeus rescued him from the lightning bolt
And brought the newborn as a god to Olympos,
Queen Hera wanted to fling him out of heaven;
So Zeus devised a counterplan, with the ingenuity worthy of
    a god.
He broke off a portion of the earth-encircling sky,
Made a decoy and handed it to Hera as a pledge of future
    good behavior.
Meanwhile he gave the real child to the nymphs to rear, and
    thus saved
Dionysos from the jealousy of Hera. As time went on,
Confusing the word sky with thigh, mortals said he was
    stitched into
The thigh of Zeus, they concocted a myth.
This god is also fortune-teller to the other gods; for
    bacchants
And maniacs have great prophetic power;
When the god enters a body with full force,
He makes those he maddens predict what is to come.
And he has also appropriated a portion of the war-god's
    province;
For when an armored host in battle formation
Takes to its heels in fear before anyone even touches a spear,
This panic comes from Dionysos.
You'll see him now and then on the rocks of Delphi
Springing with torches between the twin peaks,
Swinging and shaking the Bacchic joyrod,
Soon to be renowned through Greece.
Take care, Pentheus

Do not boast that human affairs can be controlled by force;
If you come up with an idea and that idea's a lame one, do

not
Mistake it for true wisdom. Welcome the god to the land.
Pour out libations and put ivy on your head. Bacchick it up!
As for women's self-control in matters of sex,
That's got nothing to do with Dionysos but with human
   nature.
Look facts in the face.
Even at a ritual orgy, a chaste woman will not be corrupted.
Don't you get it? You're overjoyed when a crowd gathers
At the gates and the city praises the name of Pentheus.
He too, I would imagine, delights in being honored;
Which is why Kadmos and I, whom you mock,
Crown ourselves with ivy and head for the dance,
A couple of old-timers, but we're going to trip the light
   fantastic all the same.
And I won't let you talk me into resisting the god,
For you are deranged, pitifully deranged, and there's no
Cure for your disease, no drugs or any other treatment.

CHORUS

Old man, Apollo would approve your words,
You are wise to honor Bellowing Bromios, one of the greater
   gods.

KADMOS

My boy, Teiresias has given you good advice.
Join our team, don't live outside the laws.
Right now you're all worked up, and you're not making
   sense.
Even if he isn't a god, to quote your words ,
Go ahead and say he is; tell a white lie,
Say he is Semele's son, for if people believe she gave birth to
   a god,
It can only reflect credit on our whole family.
Remember the awful fate of Aktaion

The raw-meat-eating hounds whom he had reared
Tore him asunder, for boasting in the mountain glades
That he was a better huntsman than the goddess Artemis.
Don't you suffer the same fate. Come here, my boy,

And let me crown your head with ivy.
Come with us and do honor to the god.

### PENTHEUS

Keep your hands off me, go on, go and bacchick it up,
But I'll thank you not to infect me with any of your foolery.
As for the one who taught you this folly
He shall be punished. Quick, somebody, go
To the place where this man tells fortunes by birds.
Take a crowbar, tear it down and smash it up,
Wreck it till it's one unholy mess
And throw his priestly prayer-shawls to the stormy winds.
That's the way to hurt him where he lives.
The rest of you go through the city and track down
This effeminate-looking stranger who spreads a new disease
Among the women and violates our beds.
And when you lay hands on him, bring him here
In chains, so he may get his just deserts,
Death by stoning, dancing his painful last dance in Thebes.

### TEIRESIAS

O reckless boy, you know not what you say.
Before you were simply thoughtless, but now you're stark
    raving mad.
Let's be on our way, Kadmos, and pray
To the new god on his behalf, wild man that he is,
And supplicate the god to do nothing abnormal
To the city. Lead the way with your ivied wand,
And help support my body as I support yours;
For two old men falling flat on their faces would be a sorry
    sight to see;
Come what may, we're in thrall to Bakkhos son of Zeus.
I hope Pentheus won't bring disaster on this house
Of yours, Kadmos; not that I'm prophesying, mind you.
Facts are facts, and the fool speaks folly.

## STASIMON I

CHORUS

Virtue queen of the gods
Virtue grazing the face of the earth
With golden wing,
Do you hear the words of Pentheus?
Do you hear his impure
Arrogance against Bellowing Bromios, son of
Semele, the prosperous god
First of the blest to receive
Wreaths at festivals?
The god whose custom it is
To join in the dances of his throng;
To revel in the music of flutes;
To put an end to cares,
Whenever the gleaming wine
Is served at the feasts of the gods,
And at ivy-crowned festivals
The punchbowl puts men
To sleep.

Loose lips
And lawless stupidity
Will come to a bad end;
Whereas a peaceful
Life and common sense
Are solid foundations to
Keep a house in order

For even though they dwell
Far off in the firmament,
Heaven's children keep a watchful eye on human beings.
Cleverness is not wisdom
And thinking thoughts not fit for mortals
Shortens life. With such a brief span
Who would pursue greatness and
Miss what lies at hand? Yet such
Are the habits of mortals, who
Are, as I see it, mad and
Ill-advised.

Let me go to Kypris,
Isle of the Love Goddess,
Haunt of erotic deities,
Who beguile the
Human heart,
Or let me dwell in Paphos irrigated
Without rain by the waters of the outlandish
River with its hundred mouths.
Or let me go to Pieria,
Most beauteous seat of the muses,
The sacred slope of Olympos,
There lead me, Bellowing Bromios, Bellowing Bromios,
   bacchant-leading
Spirit of joyful outcry.
There dwell the Graces.
There dwells Desire, along with the Bakkhai your chosen
   ones,
Free there to join in your orgies.
O the spirit, o the child of Zeus
Delights in celebrations
And loves the bliss-bestowing
Goddess Peace, preserver of youth.
In equal measure to rich
And poor alike he has given
The joy of wine, that solvent of sorrow;
And he abhors the man who thinks any way but this—
By daylight and by comforting darkness
To live to its end a life of bliss
And to sustain the heart and mind in true wisdom
Avoiding men who reject the ways of custom;
Whatever the crowd
Of ordinary people has taken as its rule
And practice, that's the life for me.

## SECOND EPISODE

GUARD

Pentheus, though we left in haste, we do not come back
  empty-handed.
We bring the wild beast you sent us to catch.
But we found this wild beast tame, he made no move
To run away, but voluntarily offered us his hands,
He did not pale, or blanch the wine-flushed color in his
  cheeks,
But with a laugh permitted us to bind him and lead him
  away,
Stood still, making my task an easy one.
So in my embarrassment I said, "O stranger, it's not on my
  own
Initiative I arrest you, but at the behest of Pentheus. I follow
  orders."
But as for those Bakkhai you imprisoned and
Clapped in chains behind bars in the common jail,
They have escaped, run off to the meadows
Skipping and calling upon their god Bellowing Bromios.
All by themselves their chains were loosed from their feet
And the bolts of the doors opened without human hand.
Chock-full of miracles is the man who has come here
To Thebes. Whatever happens next is your worry, not mine.

PENTHEUS

Loose his hands. Now that he is in my toils
He is not so nimble as to get away from me.
Well, your body is far from deformed, stranger,
Or so a woman might judge, for that's why you came to
  Thebes;
And your locks are long, proving you no wrestler,
They spill down your cheeks, ever so alluring;
And your skin is white by some cunning contrivance,
Not tanned by the sun, but groomed in darkness,
Where you cruise for sex with your good looks for bait.
Tell me first: who's your family, where are you from?

DIONYSOS

Not a hard question, no high marks for answering it.
Ever heard of the flower-trimmed hill-country Tmolos?

PENTHEUS

I know it, it runs in a circle round the city of Sardis.

DIONYSOS

That's where I'm from, and Lydia is my homeland.

PENTHEUS

And where did you pick up these rites you've brought to
Greece?

DIONYSOS

Dionysos initiated us, the son of Zeus himself.

PENTHEUS

Is there some Zeus in your parts who breeds new gods?

DIONYSOS

No, he's the same one who took Semele to wife here.

PENTHEUS

And were you dreaming or wide awake when he put this
spell on you?

DIONYSOS

Face to face, he inducted me into the rites.

PENTHEUS

And these orgies of yours, what are they like?

DIONYSOS

They may not be described to the uninitiate.

PENTHEUS

What pleasures do you take in these ceremonies?

DIONYSOS

Things not meant for your ears, though they are worth the knowing.

PENTHEUS

You framed that answer cleverly, to make me want to hear more.

DIONYSOS

The rituals of the god will not yield to infidels and the unholy.

PENTHEUS

Well, since you say you saw the god clearly, what was he like?

DIONYSOS

Whatever he wished to be; it wasn't up to me.

PENTHEUS

Deftly side-stepped again—with an empty phrase!

DIONYSOS

Wisdom spoken to an ignoramus never sounds like sense.

PENTHEUS

Is this the first place you've brought this god?

DIONYSOS

Every foreigner dances in these rites.

PENTHEUS

Because foreigners are barbarians, dumber than Greeks.

DIONYSOS

Wiser perhaps in this, although their ways are different.

PENTHEUS

Do you celebrate your rites by day or night?

DIONYSOS

Mostly by night; darkness lends dignity.

PENTHEUS

And sneakiness and depravity in seducing women.

DIONYSOS

Worse things may be seen by daylight.

PENTHEUS

You shall pay the price for these devious sophistries.

DIONYSOS

And you for your blindness and blasphemy.

PENTHEUS

What a big bad Bakkhos-lover, he's spent time in the debate club.

DIONYSOS

Tell me what am I to suffer? What terrible things have you got in store for me?

PENTHEUS

Well, for starters I'll cut off your cutesy curls.

DIONYSOS

My curls are sanctified; I keep them long for the god's sake.

PENTHEUS

Next, you'll drop that joyrod.

DIONYSOS

Take it yourself; it belongs to Dionysos.

PENTHEUS

Your body will be confined behind bars, under heavy guard.

DIONYSOS

The god himself will free me, whenever I wish it.

PENTHEUS

Yes, when you and the rest of the Bakkhos-lovers huddle
together and whine to him.

DIONYSOS

Since he is here now, close by, he sees what I suffer.

PENTHEUS

And just where is he, eh? He is not visible to my eyes.

DIONYSOS

Where I am. But being a godless blasphemer, you cannot see
him.

PENTHEUS

Seize him! He mocks me and Thebes in my person.

DIONYSOS

Being of sound mind, I say to you who is not of sound mind,
Do not give orders for them to bind me.

PENTHEUS

I'm the one in charge here, and I order them to bind you.

DIONYSOS

You have no idea what your life means or what you're doing
or who you are.

PENTHEUS

Pentheus, son of Agaue and my father Echion.

DIONYSOS

An appropriate name: is not penthos Greek for cruel pain?

PENTHEUS

Get him out of here! Confine him nearby in some horse
Stall, so that he may look on dusky darkness.
Try your fancy footwork in the stables; and as for those
women you brought here
As co-conspirators in your depravity,
We'll either sell them or, now that I've stopped

Their hands from this pounding, this drum-beating,
I'll place them as domestic slaves at the looms.

DIONYSOS

I am ready to go. For if a thing is not fated to happen, I
  cannot
Suffer by it. As for these arrogant actions of yours, Dionysos
  will call
You to account, Dionysos the god you say does not exist.
For, when you do us wrong, he is the one you lead away in
  chains.


# STASIMON II

CHORUS

Daughter of Acheloüs,
Queen river Dirké, a maiden blest,
For once you bathed Zeus's offspring
In your waters
When Zeus his begetter snatched him from the flames,
Hid him in his thigh,
Calling out
"Come, my boy, my song of joy, crawl into my
Masculine womb;
When I reveal you
To Thebes, o Bakkhos, let it call you by this name."
But you, o blessed Dirké,
You drive me off, though I bring
Garlands and I stage revels on your banks.
Why do you spurn me? Why do you run from me?
Yea, soon enough, stimulated by the joy of clustering grapes,
Dionysos's wine,
You'll pay some heed to Bellowing Bromios.

What rage, what rage
He displays, Pentheus, whose father was
The old dragon's seed,
Echion sprung from the Earth.
He behaves like a wild-eyed monster, not of
Human breed, like a murderous

Giant contending with the gods.
Who dares put me in chains,
Me a handmaid of Bellowing Bromios,
Who dares confine me with
My companions already
Mewed up in a dismal dungeon?

Do you see these things, o son of Zeus,
Dionysos, your followers
Struggling with repression?
Come, Lord, down from Olympos,
Brandishing your gold-headed joyrod,
And check the violent arrogance of this bloodthirsty man.

O where is your wand waving
Over the rites, o Dionysos?
On Mount Nyssa, nurse-maid of
Wild beasts, or
On the slopes of Korykos?
Perhaps in the well-wooded
Groves of Olympos, where
Once Orpheus, strumming his lyre,
Set the trees tripping to his tune,
Called together the beasts of the wilderness.
O blessed Pieria,
The god to whom we cry Euoi adores you, he shall
Partner the Bakkhai in their dances,
And across the swift-flowing
Axios he shall lead
The swirling maenads,
And across Lydias,
Bringer of bliss
To fortunate mortals,
The father of rivers, who, so goes the tale,
Enriches a land of pedigreed steeds
With the fairest of waters.

# THIRD EPISODE

### DIONYSOS

Io, hear, hear me calling,
Io Bakkhai, Io Bakkhai.

### CHORUS

What do I hear, what is this cry, where is it from,
Why does the god who is hailed by cries of Euoi, hail me?

### DIONYSOS

Io, Io, again I cry,
Hear the son of Semele and Zeus.

### CHORUS

Io, Io, master, master,
Come now to our
Band of revellers, o Bellowing Bromios, Bromios Bellowing.

### DIONYSOS

Rattle the floor of the world, sovereign spirit of Earthquake.

### CHORUS

Ah, ah,
In an instant the house of Pentheus
Will be shaken to its fall.
O Dionysos invades the house;
O come let us adore him. —O we do adore him.
Did you see how those stone lintels gaped
Atop those pillars? It is Bellowing Bromios making those
Inside the walls cry out in distress.

### DIONYSOS

Kindle the red-hot torch of lightning.
Burn, burn down the house of Pentheus.

### CHORUS

Ah, ah,
Do you not see the fire, not behold
About the holy tomb of Semele, the flame

Once ignited by Zeus's lightning
Emitted by his thunder-bolt?
Hurl hard to the ground your trembling body,
Maenads; for Our Lord
Assails this house, turning it upside-down,
Our Lord, the son of God.

### DIONYSOS

Women of Asia, are you so filled with fear
That you fall to the ground? I suppose you felt Bakkhos
Shaking the house of Pentheus; but lift up
Your bodies and take heart, put off this trembling of the
flesh.

### CHORUS

O guiding light of our joyous, clamorous revels,
How glad I am to see you in my abandoned desperation.

### DIONYSOS

Did you lose heart when I was led away,
Thinking I'd languish in the dark dungeons of Pentheus?

### CHORUS

How could I help it? Who will protect me if you meet with
    disaster?
But how did you free yourself after your encounter with that
    ungodly man?

### DIONYSOS

I came as salvation unto myself, no big deal.

### CHORUS

But weren't your hands tied tight with knotted ropes?

### DIONYSOS

I hoodwinked him there too, for thinking he had hogtied me
He never bothered to touch or hold me, but lived on
    illusions.
Inside the stables, where he led me and expected to confine
    me, he found
A bull, and lassoed its knees and hooves with his rope,

Panting in his anger, gnawing his lips,
His body dripping sweat;
While I stood right beside him and
Coolly, calmly watched the show.
And in the meantime
Bakkhos came and shook the house, and his mother's tomb
Caught fire; and that man, thinking his house was ablaze,
Ran up and down, ordering the servants to bring water from
The river, but no matter how hard his slaves toiled, their
    work was all in vain.
Then, pausing in his task, suspecting that I had escaped,
He drew his dark sword and rushed inside the house.
But Bellowing Bromios, or so I think—I'm only guessing
    here—
Conjured up a phantasm of light in the courtyard; and the
    king, rushing at it in his frenzy,
Thrust and stabbed at the shining vapor, thinking that he
    spilled my blood.
Bakkhos had other ways of humiliating him as well
He razed the house to the ground; and all is shattered;
Pentheus saw a most painful (or should I say Penthful?) end
    to my imprisonment;
And in his distress, exhausted, he collapsed and dropped his
    sword;
After all, being nothing but a man he dared wage war on a
    god.
So, quietly leaving the house, I came to you, caring not a rap
    for Pentheus.
Yet if I'm not mistaken (for I do hear a footfall within the
    house)
He'll be out here any minute now. What do you think he'll
    say after all this?
Oh well, I'll take him in my stride, even if he comes
    breathing fire and brimstone.
For a wise man knows how to exercise self-control and never
    lose his temper.

PENTHEUS
I have been through hell. The stranger got away,
Even though he was tied hand and foot.

A-ah, a-ah!
There he is! What's going on here? How can you be standing
In front of my house, in the open air?

#### DIONYSOS

Don't take another step! And rein in your temper as well!

#### PENTHEUS

How did you manage to escape and get outside?

#### DIONYSOS

Didn't I say—or didn't you hear—that a certain somebody
  would free me?

#### PENTHEUS

Who? For you made so many irrelevant remarks.

#### DIONYSOS

He who grows the fruit of the vine for mortals.

#### PENTHEUS

Now there's a real benefit to humanity.

#### DIONYSOS

You insult the glory of Dionysos.

#### PENTHEUS

I command every tower in the circle to be locked and bolted.

#### DIONYSOS

So what? Can't gods get over walls?

#### PENTHEUS

Clever, clever, I admit you're clever, except where it really
  counts.

#### DIONYSOS

Where it really and truly counts is where I am naturally
  clever.
But first learn something from the words of this man
Who comes from the mountain with a message for you;

We will stand waiting on your convenience. We won't run
  away.

MESSENGER

Pentheus ruler of this Theban land,
I have come from Mount Kithairon, where
The gleaming white snowdrifts never thaw and melt.

PENTHEUS

And what message do you bring that can't wait?

MESSENGER

Now that I've seen the Bakkhos-crazed women, who in their
  delirium
Darted from this land, flashing their white limbs,
I have come eager to tell you and the city, sire,
Of their weird carryings-on and more than miracles.
But I've got to know whether I may speak my piece freely
Or put a clamp on my tongue;
For I fear your all too royal temper, sire,
Its rashness and its harshness.

PENTHEUS

Speak, you may speak with impunity, whatever your story.
It is wrong to take offense at those in the right.
But the uglier the things you say about the Bakkhai,
The uglier the penalty we shall impose
On the man who put such practices into the heads of the
  crazy women.

MESSENGER

The grazing herds of young calves were just
Climbing upland to the mountaintop, at the hour when the
  sun
Lets loose its warming beams upon the earth
When I see three bands of woman revellers,
One led by Autonoë, the second
By your mother Agaue, and the third set of dancers by Ino.
And all of them asleep, their bodies relaxed,
Some stretched out on their backs against pine-tree boughs,
Some resting their heads on the ground pillowed by oak

leaves,
Higgledy-piggledy, but modestly, not, as you might think,
Drunk from punch bowls, boozy in the great outdoors, or
Hunting for sex to the sound of the flute.
Then your mother stood up amidst the Bakkhai
And howled, to rouse their bodies from sleep,
For she'd heard the lowing of the hornèd cattle.
And rubbing the sand of slumber from their eyes
They staggered to their feet, a strange sight in its ordered
     calm,
Young women and old and maidens yet unmarried,
And first they let down their hair upon their shoulders
And hiked up the fawn-skins which had come loose
From their binding knots, and fastened the dappled hide
With serpents that licked their cheeks.
And some held an antelope in their arms and wolves' cubs
Wild and let them suck white milk,
Those recent mothers whose breasts were bursting
And who had left their babes at home; and they put on ivy
Crowns and oak and flowering evergreen.
And one of them took her joyrod and struck it on a rock,
And from it spurted a dewy stream of water;
And another struck her wand upon the ground,
And the god sent forth a fountain of his wine;
And those who had a craving for the white drink,
Clawed the ground with finger nails, and
They got streams of milk; and from the ivy
Wands dripped rivulets of sweet honey.
So that, if you had been there and had seen this,
You would supplicate in prayer the god you now disparage.
Then we cowherds and shepherds gathered together
In solemn conclave to pool our observations of
Their weird behavior and fantastic doings;
And one fellow who used to hang out in town and has a
knack for public speaking
Said to the rest of us: "O residents of the stately mountain
Pastures, what do you say we chase
Pentheus's mother Agaue from the bacchic revels
And so gain favor with his majesty?" We all figured he was
On to something, so we lay in ambush, hiding

In the bushy thickets. And at the appointed hour
They brought the magic joyrods to the bacchic rites,
Calling in unison upon Bellowing Bromios the son of Zeus;
And the whole mountain and its beasts
Were god-possessed, and all things took part in the general
    upheaval.
Now it so happened that Agaue was capering beside me,
And I leaped up to try and get hold of her,
Abandoning the bushes where I had been hiding.
But she cried out: "O hounds that run with me,
We are hunted by these men; follow me,
Follow and arm yourselves with the joyrods in your hands."
So we hightailed it out of there, and so avoided
Being torn to pieces by the crazed women, for they fell on
    the
Grazing heifers with their unarmed hands.
You should have seen one of these maniacs take a bellowing
    calf
With distended udder in her two hands,
While others wrenched asunder full-grown heifers.
And you should have seen the rib cages and cloven hooves
Scattered all over the place; and gobbets of flesh seemed to
    hang
From the pine-trees dripping blood.
Bulls, that used to be aggressive, with anger
Seated in their horns, toppled to the ground,
Dragged down by the countless hands of girls.
And those girls stripped them of the garment of flesh
Faster than you could wink your royal eyes.
Then, moving like birds, upborne by their own speed,
They cross the stretch of plain, along Asopus stream
Which produces fertile grain for Thebes,
And swooping down like enemy warriors
On to Hysiai and Erythrai, villages at the foothills of
    Kithairon,
They destroy everything high and low.
They snatched children from their homes;
Whatever they put on their shoulders balanced there
    without falling,
Heavy bronze or iron vessels, without the use of cords; and

in their curls
Fire flashed, but did not burn. Then the villagers, angry
At being plundered by the crazed women, took up arms.
Now there was a dreadful sight to see, sire,
For the blades of the men's spears could not draw blood,
Whereas the women loosed the joyrods from their hands
And wounded them and made them turn tail and run,—
Women did this to men, some god must have had a hand in
   it.
And then they moved back to where they'd started out,
To the streams their god had made for them.
And they washed off the blood, and the drops on the skin
Of their cheeks were licked away by the tongues of serpents.
Which means, this god, whoever he may be, o sire,
Welcome him to this city; for he is great in other things too,
For people say, or so the story goes,
He gave to mortals the vine that puts an end to suffering.
And if there were no more wine, there'd be no more
   lovemaking,
Or any other pleasure for mankind.

CHORUS

I fear to speak my mind
To a tyrant, but it must be said
Dionysos is second to no other god.

PENTHEUS

Now this bacchic insolence, this violence
Flares up like brushfire in our neighborhood,
And puts all Greece to shame.
We've got no time to spare; go at once to the Elektran
Gate; summon all the heavy infantry
And muster all the cavalry on fleet-footed steeds,
And the light infantry and have the archers
Tighten their bowstrings, for we shall march against
The Bakkhai. Things have got entirely out of hand
If we have to put up with such nonsense—and from women
at that!

DIONYSOS

You've heard what I've had to say, Pentheus,
And yet it goes right past you. Even though you've
    mistreated me,
I advise you not take up arms against a god,
But to keep calm; Bellowing Bromios will not allow
You to drive his followers from the hills of joyful clamor.

PENTHEUS

Stop lecturing me! You have broken jail;
Take care you hold on to your freedom—
Or would you rather I renewed your punishment?

DIONYSOS

I'd make him an offering instead of losing your temper
And taking a stand against his provocations, a mortal man
    versus a god.

PENTHEUS

An offering? Yes, of women's blood, just what they deserve.
I'll spill it with an open hand throughout Kithairon's glens.

DIONYSOS

You will all be put to flight; what a disgrace, to have your
    shields
Of beaten bronze turned aside by the joyrods of Bakkhos-
    crazed women.

PENTHEUS

This stranger has me in a stranglehold. How do you deal
With someone who won't shut up in jail or at liberty?

DIONYSOS

My good sir, there is still a way to bring about a happy
    ending.

PENTHEUS

By doing what? Being a slave to my slaves?

DIONYSOS

I shall bring the women here without the use of weapons.

PENTHEUS

Here we go again! This is some trick to hoodwink me.

DIONYSOS

What do you mean trick, since I wish to save you by my
skills?

PENTHEUS

You and the women have worked out some arrangement,
So you can go on revelling forever.

DIONYSOS

True enough, I did work out an arrangement—but with the
god.

PENTHEUS

Bring me my weapons, and you keep your trap shut.

DIONYSOS

Ah!
Would you like to see them sprawling there on the
mountain-side?

PENTHEUS

Indeed I would! I 'd give uncounted gold to see that.

DIONYSOS

Why, I wonder, do you have such a great craving for this?

PENTHEUS

I should be sorry to see them drunk.

DIONYSOS

And yet you're eager to see something that would give you
pain?

PENTHEUS

Of course, but secretly, crouched in the shadow of the
pines.

DIONYSOS

But they may sniff you out, even if you come in secret.

PENTHEUS

In the open then; you are right about that.

DIONYSOS

Then may we be your guide, will you undertake the
journey?

PENTHEUS

Lead on without delay! I'll make you pay for wasted time.

DIONYSOS

First you must clothe your body in a robe of oriental linen.

PENTHEUS

What's this? I'm to give up my manhood and be
downgraded to a woman?

DIONYSOS

Or else they'll kill you, once they know a man's around.

PENTHEUS

Another good point! What a clever fellow you are, but then
you always were.

DIONYSOS

It comes of studying with Dionysos.

PENTHEUS

So what's the best way to follow your good advice?

DIONYSOS

I shall dress you, inside the house.

PENTHEUS

What dress? Woman's wear? But that would be humiliating!

DIONYSOS

Then you've changed your mind and don't care to observe the maenads?

PENTHEUS

What precisely do you suggest I put on my body?

DIONYSOS

I will attach long hair to your head.

PENTHEUS

And what's the next item in my make-over?

DIONYSOS

Skirts down to your feet; and on your head a turban.

PENTHEUS

And what will you give me for accessories?

DIONYSOS

A joyrod in your hand and a dappled fawnskin stole.

PENTHEUS

I would never be able to wear women's clothes.

DIONYSOS

But if you rush to attack the Bakkhai blood will be shed.

PENTHEUS

You are right; I must first reconnoiter.

DIONYSOS

That's a wiser course than to fight fire with fire.

PENTHEUS

And how am I to go through Kadmos's city unobserved?

DIONYSOS

We'll take back alleys; and I will lead the way.

PENTHEUS

Anything, rather than have those Bakkhos-crazed women
  gloating over me in triumph.

DIONYSOS

Why not go in the house then?...

PENTHEUS

I have yet to determine the best course of action.

DIONYSOS

As you like; whatever you decide, I am ready and willing,
close at hand.

PENTHEUS

I think I will go inside. Either I'll march at the head of an
army
Or I'll be persuaded by your advice.

DIONYSOS

Women, the man is caught in the toils of the net,
And he shall visit the Bakkhai, where he will pay the penalty
  of death.
Dionysos, now it is up to you; for you are close at hand;
Take your revenge. But first distract his mind,
Implant a dizzy fantasy; for if his mind's on the right track
He'll never agree to wear a woman's dress,
Whereas driven down a mental detour he will.
I want to turn him into a laughingstock for the Thebans,
As he is led in female finery through the city,
Sharp contrast to his earlier threats, when he tried to be so
  awe-inspiring.
Now I'm off to dress Pentheus in the ensemble
He will be wearing when he goes to Hell,
Butchered by his mother's hand;
And then he shall acknowledge Dionysos the son of Zeus,
Born to be a god most terrible in the mystic ritual
But most gentle to mankind.

## STASIMON III

When, o when shall I set
My bare white feet dancing the all-night revels,
Flinging back my head in ecstasy
In the dew-drenched air?
Like a fawn at play in
The verdant joy of meadows,
After she has escaped the panic of the hunt,
Clear of the circling beaters,
Beyond the tightly-woven nets,

And the hallooing huntsman
Urging on his harried hounds
With tension redoubled,
And she sprints, racing with storm-swift bursts of energy,
To the water-meadow,
Delighting in a landscape empty of men,
And in the green buds that shoot up
Shadowed by the forest leaves.

What is wisdom? Or what gift of the gods
Is sweeter in men's opinion
Than to hold the upper hand
Over a fallen foe?
Why, 'tis a thing of beauty
And a joy forever.

Grinding slowly but unerringly
The power of the gods proceeds.
It brings to book those mortals
Headstrong in their heedlessness
And deluded in their pride,
Who will not render unto God the things that are God's.
The gods are devious in their ways,
Concealing the unhurried march of time
As they track down the unbeliever.
Never should one's thoughts, one's actions
Go beyond traditional beliefs.
It costs so little

To make this your creed
Whatever is divine is strong;
Whatever has been sanctioned by long practice
Is a law eternal and
Rooted deep in nature.

What is wisdom? Or what gift of the gods
Is sweeter in men's opinion
Than to hold the upper hand
Over a fallen foe?
Why, 'tis a thing of beauty
And a joy forever.

Happy the man who survives a storm at sea,
And comes safe home to harbor.
Happy the man who sinks under affliction and comes out in
    one piece.
In all sorts of ways one man outpaces another in the
Race for wealth and power.
Ten thousand men cherish ten thousand several hopes for
    the future.
A few may achieve prosperity in this life; the others may fall
    short.
But the man who takes each moment's happiness as it comes
    I call truly blest.

## FOURTH EPISODE

### DIONYSOS

You who are so eager to spy on what should not be spied on
And long for what should not be longed for, in other words
    Pentheus,
Come out of the house, let me have a look at you,
Decked out in the trappings of a woman, a follower of
Bakkhos, a crazed maenad,
And a voyeur of your mother and her gang;
Why, you look like one of Kadmos's daughters.

PENTHEUS

I seem to see two suns in the sky,
And a double Thebes the seven-gated city;
And I get the impression you are a bull walking ahead of me
And I think your head has sprouted horns.
Were you an animal all this time? For certainly now you are
   changed to a bull.

DIONYSOS

The god, who used to be hostile to you, now walks with us
As a peace-offering; consequently your vision has been
   corrected.

PENTHEUS

Well, how do I look? Wouldn't you say the spitting image of
   Aunt Ino
Or my mother Agaue?

DIONYSOS

You could have fooled me.
But a curl has come loose from its place,
Let me tuck it beneath your turban as I did before.

PENTHEUS

In the house, rocking my head back and forth
And rolling with Bacchic joy I must have shaken it loose.

DIONYSOS

Then let me serve as your dresser and
Re-arrange it. But do keep your head straight.

PENTHEUS

Come on! Smarten me up! I put myself entirely in your
hands.

DIONYSOS

Your girdle is slack, and the pleats of your skirt
Hang crooked below your ankle.

PENTHEUS

I think so too, on the right side, wouldn't you say?
But on the left the dress clings casually to my calf.

DIONYSOS

You are going to call me your very best friend,
When, counter to all expectations, you see how well-behaved
  the Bakkhai are.

PENTHEUS

Should I hold the joyrod in my right hand
Or the left, which looks more like a follower of Bakkhos?

DIONYSOS

You must raise it in your right hand, in time
With your right foot. I congratulate you on your change of
  mind.

PENTHEUS

Will I be able to lift the forests of Kithairon
And all the Bakkhai on my shoulders?

DIONYSOS

You could if you wanted to; before you were not in your
Right mind, but now your mind is all it should be.

PENTHEUS

Should we take crowbars? Or should I tear up the cliffs with
  my bare hands,
Putting my shoulders or my arms to their crags.

DIONYSOS

Would you destroy the shrines of the nymphs
And the seat of Pan where he does his piping?

PENTHEUS

You're right; women should not be conquered
By brute force; I shall hide in the shadow of the pine-trees.

DIONYSOS

You shall hide in just the sort of hiding-place fit for
A peeping Tom who would keep secret watch on maenads.

PENTHEUS

Imagine! I can picture them now in the bushes,
Naked as jay-birds, hugging tight in the voluptuous tangles
  of hot sex.

DIONYSOS

Quite right, your mission is to be a one-man vice squad.
No doubt you'll catch them in the dirty deed, if they don't
  catch you first.

PENTHEUS

Parade me down the main streets of Thebes;
For only I am man enough to dare this deed.

DIONYSOS

Only you bear the burden for this city, you alone;
Which is why the appropriate ordeals are in store for you.
Follow me; I am your guide and safeguard on the way there,
But someone else will bring you back again.

PENTHEUS

The woman who gave me birth.

DIONYSOS

As an example to all.

PENTHEUS

That's why I go.

DIONYSOS

You shall be carried home...

PENTHEUS

That sounds like deluxe treatment.

DIONYSOS

In your mother's arms.

PENTHEUS

You insist on pampering me to pieces.

DIONYSOS

To pieces, yes—in my own peculiar way.

PENTHEUS

I go to claim my just reward.

DIONYSOS

You're a very special person and you're about to have a very
    special experience,
Which will bring you a fame towering to heaven.
Stretch out your arms, Agaue and you her sisters,
Daughters of Kadmos; I escort this youth
To a great contest, whose winners will be myself
And Bellowing Bromios. Wait and see what happens next.

## STASIMON IV

CHORUS

Run to the mountain, fleet hounds of Frenzy!
Run to the revels of Kadmos's daughters.
Goad them to madness against the cross-dresser,
The voyeur who spies on the Maenads. As he peeks at them
From behind some sheer rock or vantage point his mother
Will be the first to catch sight of him. She will rally
The Maenads, calling: "Who is this tracker of
"Mountain-dancing daughters of Kadmos?
"What creature engendered him, Bakkhai?
"This man is not of woman born, but birthed by
"Some she-lion, the Libyan gorgons bred such a brute!"

O Justice, show yourself; stalk him with a sword.
Stab home to the throat that godless, lawless, conscienceless
    man,
The spawn of earth-born Echion.

He's setting forth, the infidel, untamed and
Mutinous, berserk and blinded by bigotry,
Insanely assailing the mystic rites of the god,

Profaning the rites of the god's mother.
Frantically he butts against the invincible,
Hoping to overcome it by violence.
Death will humble him. The gods deal out death
To teach us moderation, to remind us that we are not gods.
To recall our mortality is to free us of anxiety.
I do not envy the wise their wisdom;
I take pleasure in hunting those other spoils,
Those great and obvious goals which channel
Life towards the finer things—
To be pious and reverent, by day and by night,
To avoid behavior that lies outside tradition,
To honor the gods.
O Justice, show yourself; stalk him with a sword.
Stab home to the throat that godless, lawless, conscienceless
    man,
The spawn of earth-born Echion.
O Dionysos, show yourself to us as a bull.
Or a snake with darting heads, a lion snorting fire.
Let us see you in those forms.
O Bakkhos, come. Come with smiling face and
Cast your deadly noose about this man who hunts
Your Bakkhai, when he's crushed beneath the stampede of
    your myriad Maenads!


# FIFTH EPISODE

### Messenger 2

O halls which once were happy in the eyes of all Greece,
O race of the Sidonian ancient who sowed
The earth-born crop of dragon-seed,
How I groan for you, slave though I am, but still
Good slaves can sympathize with their master's calamities.

### Chorus

What is it? What news do you bring of the Bakkhos-crazed
    women?

MESSENGER 2

Pentheus, son of Echion, is dead.

CHORUS

O Lord Bromios the Bellower, your divinity is revealed!

MESSENGER 2

What are you talking about? Why do you say such things?
Are you rejoicing, woman, at the misfortunes of my
    deceased master?

CHORUS

I am a foreigner and cry in ecstasy to a barbarian tune.
No longer do I cower in fear of chains.

MESSENGER 2

Do you consider Thebes so poor in men—

CHORUS

O Dionysos, Dionysos, Thebes
Has no power over me.

MESSENGER 2

This behavior of yours may be excused, nevertheless, o
    women,
It is not becoming to rejoice at evil deeds.

CHORUS

Tell me, speak, by what doom did he die,
The unjust man, inventor of injustice?

MESSENGER 2

When we had left the outskirts of the Theban town,
And forded the streams of Asopus,
We struck into the hill-country round Kithairon,
Pentheus and I—for I followed my master,—
And the stranger who was our guide to the things we were
    to see.
And so we first concealed ourselves in tall grass in a glen,
Stilling every move of foot or tongue
So we might see but not be seen.

There lay a grove, cliff-bound, refreshed with waters,
Overshadowed by pines, where the maenads
Sat employing their hands in pleasant crafts.
For some of them were restoring the crown,
The frayed ivy locks on a dishevelled joyrod,
And others, frisky as fillies freed from painted yokes,
Were singing madrigals to Bacchic melodies.
But Pentheus, wretched man, unable to see this female
    crowd,
Said: "O stranger, from where we stand,
My vision cannot reach these crazed, hysteric women;
But if I climb a tall pine-tree on the banks of the ravine
I can get a clear view of the maenads' obscene antics."
And right then and there I see the stranger make a miracle;
For seizing the sky-high top of a pine-tree
He pulled it down, down, down to the dark earth;
And it was curved as a bow is bent or as a round wheel
Comes full-circle when its rim has been traced by a compass;
This was how the stranger, pulling with his hands,
Bent the mountain tree to earth, doing no human deed.
And seating Pentheus on the pine branches,
He released the trunk through his hands
Not letting it wobble, taking care it should not throw him,
And sheer into the sheer air it towered,
With my master astride its back.
But he was more visible to the maenads than they were to
    him.
And no sooner did they begin to see him riding high,
Than the stranger disappeared,
And some voice from the sky, could be it was
Dionysos's, cried out, "O young women,
I bring you the man who makes a mockery
Of me and you and the sacred mysteries;
Take your revenge on him."
And then as the voice spoke these words, a flash of fearful
    fire
Shot up between earth and heaven.
And the air above fell still, and the leaves of the wooded
    glade ceased
To rustle, and no beast made a sound.

But the women, who had not heard the voice clearly,
Stood up straight and gazed about them.
And again it called out, and when they distinctly
Heard the command of Bakkhos, Kadmos's daughters,
As swift as any startled dove,
Sped away, their feet taut with running,
His mother Agaue and her kith and kin
And all the Bakkhai. They leapt through the torrent-flowing
    glade
And over broken rocks, maddened by the god's inspiring.
And when they saw my master perched in the pine,
First they violently hurled rocks at him,
Then, having climbed a boulder that towered across the way,
They hurtled pine branches at him like javelins,
And others tossed their joyrods through the air
At Pentheus, savage target-shooting; but they missed him.
For at a height beyond the reach of their fanaticism
The poor wretch sat, trapped with no means of escape.
Finally, they tried to pry up the roots, with levers not of iron,
But with oaken boughs, shattering them like thunderbolts.
And when, for all their effort, they could not bring him
    down,
Agaue said, "Here, stand in a circle and
Take hold of the trunk, maenads, so we can capture
This climbing beast and keep him from reporting the god's
Secret rituals." And they laid a thousand hands
On the pine-tree and yanked it out of the ground;
And from his lofty seat on high down falls
Pentheus, tumbling to the ground,
With a thousand shrieks, for he knew the end was near.
And his mother was the first to fall on the victim
Like a priestess at a sacrifice; and he snatched the turban
    from his hair
So that wretched Agaue would recognize him and not kill
Him, and he said, stroking her cheek,
"Look, mother, I am your son
Pentheus, whom you bore to my father Echion;
Pity me, mother, do not because I've
Gone astray kill your child."
But she was foaming at the mouth, her distended eyeballs

Rolling, totally out of her mind,
Possessed by Bakkhos, and he could not get through to her.
Then seizing his left arm in her hands
And setting her foot hard against the doomed man's rib-
    cage,
She wrenched his shoulder out, not with her own strength,
But the god had given her hand the cunning.
And Ino was clawing at his other side,
Rending flesh, and Autonoë and the whole crowd
Of Bakkhai went on the attack; and every throat bellowed
    together—
He screaming with what breath was left in him,
While they were cheering for victory. And one carried away
    an arm,
Another a foot still in its hunting-boot; and his ribs
Were stripped by ripping nails; and every hand was
    bloodied
As they played ball with hunks of Pentheus's flesh.
The body lies scattered, part beneath jagged
Rocks, and part among the thick-carpetted leaves of the
    forest,
No easy task to find. But his wretched head,
Which by chance his mother was still holding,
She impaled on the point of a joyrod, and she bore it
Like a mountain lion's across Mount Kithairon,

Abandoning her sisters to their orgiastic dances.
And she is coming here, within these walls,
Exulting in the gruesome quarry, calling on Bakkhos
Her fellow huntsman, her colleague in capture,
Patron of winners—but in serving him her reward will be
    tears.
Anyway, to avoid this awfulness,
I will leave before Agaue comes to the house.
To be self-effacing and to worship the gods
Is wisest; and I think this piece of wisdom the best
Gift a human being can possess.

## STASIMON 5

CHORUS

Let us dance for Bakkhos,
Let us proclaim the comeuppance
Of Pentheus, seed of the dragon;
Who put on woman's wear
And took up a joyrod imbued
By the god with special venom,
To be led by a bull to his doom.
Kadmean Bakkhai,
A magnificent hymn of triumph you have sung—
But it ends in lamentation,
It ends in tears.
A fine victory this—to glove a dripping hand
In the steaming blood of one's own child.

But I behold running to the house
Pentheus' mother Agaue, her eyes
In fine frenzy rolling,—welcome the revelling band of the
    cheer-leading god.

## EXODOS

AGAUE

Bakkhai of Asia.

CHORUS

O, why do you call on me, woman?

AGAUE

We bring from the mountains
A newly-cut tendril to deck the halls,
Our hunt was a happy one.

CHORUS

I see and I welcome you, fellow reveller.

AGAUE

Without a lasso I overcame this
Lion's whelp;
You can see for yourselves.

CHORUS

From what wild place?

AGAUE

On Mount Kithairon...

CHORUS

Kithairon?

AGAUE

I slew him.

CHORUS

Who struck the blow?

AGAUE

Mine was the first blow to be struck.
Lucky, lucky Agaue is what the revellers call me.

CHORUS

Who else was in for the kill?

AGAUE

Next Kadmos's...

CHORUS

Kadmos's what?

AGAUE

Daughters
After I did, after I did they laid
Hands on this prey; our hunting has been happy.
Now join in the feast.

CHORUS

What? You want me to join in, wretched woman?

AGAUE

The bullock's a young one;
His cheek is just growing downy
Beneath his crest of fine hair.

CHORUS

Yes, his hair does make him look like a beast of the wild.

AGAUE

O Bakkhos the huntsman
Shrewdly spurred the maenads
To the chase.

CHORUS

For the lord is our hunter, we shall not want.

AGAUE

Do you praise me?

CHORUS

I praise you indeed.

AGAUE

Soon the kinsmen of Kadmos...

CHORUS

And your son Pentheus too?...

AGAUE

Will praise his mother
For catching this wild lion-cub.

CHORUS

Strange spoil.

AGAUE

And strangely taken.

CHORUS

Do you glory in it?

AGAUE

I do glory in it,
Great, great,
Great in the sight of all is this spoil I have taken.

CHORUS

Then, o wretched woman, display to the city
The prize that you brought from the hunt.


# SIXTH EPISODE


AGAUE

O citizens of the well-towered capital of the Theban
Land, come and see this trophy of the beast
Which we daughters of Kadmos hunted down,
Not with thonged javelins of Thessaly,
Nor with nets, but with the fingers of our white hands,
Our arms our blades. What's there for a huntsman to brag
    about
If he has to rely on the spear-maker's missiles?
For with our bare hands we caught him,
And disjointed the beast limb from limb.
Where is the old man my father? Send him to me.
Where is my son Pentheus? Let him take a ladder
And place it securely against the house, so he
Can nail to the fluted beam-ends the head of this
Lion I have here, the spoil of my hunt.

KADMOS

Follow me with your burden, —put it down, attendants, in
    front of the house,—
The tormented weight of Pentheus,
Whose body I have recovered. With endless searching and
Much toil I found it in the forests of Kithairon
Rent asunder, and collected the pieces, strewn all over the
    place,
Each lying hidden deep in the woods.
For I had heard of my daughters's carryings-on,
While I was still within the city's walls, on my return

With old Teiresias from the Bacchic revels;
So turning back to the mountain, I retrieved
The child slain by the maenads.
There I saw Aristaios's wife Autonoë who once
Was mother to Aktaion, and with her Ino, still
Among the oaks, both out of their minds, poor creatures,
But Agaue, someone told me, had hotfooted it home
Crazed by Bakkhos; he didn't misinform me,
For here she is, not a pretty picture.

### AGAUE

Father, you're entitled to boast the loudest,
For you have begot the best daughters by far of all
The world; all of them without exception, and first and not
    least myself,
Who, leaving my shuttle at the loom,
Have risen to higher things, hunting beasts with my bare
    hands.
I hold in my hands, as you see, this
Trophy of valor, so that it may be hung up
In your house; now, father, take it in your hands;
And rejoicing in my hunting
Call your friends to a feast; for you are blest,
Blest, that we have done such deeds.

### KADMOS

O grief immeasurable, grief not fit to be seen in public,
The deed you have done with your hands is murder most
    foul.
A handsome quarry you have struck down, one fit for the
    gods,
And now you invite Thebes and me to feast on it.
Alas for our sufferings, first yours, then mine;
For the god, Lord Bromios the Bellower, has destroyed us
Justly perhaps, but he has gone too far, considering he is a
    member of the family.

### AGAUE

Old men are such grumblers,
Forever scowling at the world. I wish my son

Were as good a hunter as his mother,
When he and the young men of Thebes go out
To chase game; but all he can do
Is fight against the god. You should give him a scolding,
    father,
Personally. Will someone call him here so I can see him and
He can behold my good fortune?

KADMOS

Woe, woe, woe. When you become aware of what you've
    done
The pain you'll undergo will be excruciating. If you were to
    remain
Delirious permanently, no one could call you happy,
But then at least your unhappiness would not be so intense.

AGAUE

What is wrong, what do you consider so awful about this?

KADMOS

First raise your eyes to the upper air.

AGAUE

All right; but why would you have me look up?

KADMOS

Does it seem the same to you or has it changed?

AGAUE

Brighter than before and more translucent.

KADMOS

And is your mind still fogged by its hallucination?

AGAUE

I don't see what you're driving at. But my head is
    somehow…
Clearing, something in my mind has altered.

KADMOS

Then will you hear and answer clearly?

AGAUE

Yes, for I seem to have forgot what we were saying just now,
father.

KADMOS

When the wedding march played, whose house did you
come to?

AGAUE

You wed me to the man they called Dragon-seed, Echion.

KADMOS

And in that house what child did you bear your husband?

AGAUE

Pentheus, the fruit of our wedlock.

KADMOS

And whose head do you cradle in your arms?

AGAUE

A lion's,—or so the huntresses told me.

KADMOS

Well then, you must have a good long look: it only takes a
moment.

AGAUE

Ah, what do I behold? What am I holding in my hands?

KADMOS

Look closely at it and learn more surely.

AGAUE

I see the sharpest pain that I can suffer.

KADMOS

Does it still look to you like a lion?

AGAUE

No, wretch that I am, I hold the head of Pentheus.

KADMOS

Whom I mourned long before you recognized him.

AGAUE

Who killed him? —How did he get into my hands?

KADMOS

O cheerless truth, how unwelcome you are now.

AGAUE

Speak, for my heart is in my mouth with fear.

KADMOS

You killed him, and your sisters with you.

AGAUE

Where did he die? At home? Or in what place?

KADMOS

Where once Aktaion was torn to pieces by his own hounds.

AGAUE

But why did he go to Kithairon, ill-fated boy?

KADMOS

He meant to insult the god by attending your revels.

AGAUE

But what were we doing, gathered in that place?

KADMOS

You were out of your minds. The whole city had gone
Bakkhos-mad.

AGAUE

Dionysos has destroyed us, that much I recognize.

KADMOS

For being arrogant and insulting; you did not acknowledge
him a god.

AGAUE

The darling body of my child, where is it, father?

KADMOS

I had some trouble finding its scattered pieces, but here it is.

AGAUE

Is Pentheus whole? Are his limbs fitted decently in their
    proper sockets?

KADMOS

All but the head. Even so, the remains are mutilated
    horribly.

AGAUE

O father, do you see how my fortune has changed?
I'm in agonies now, when just moments ago I preened in my
    triumph,
Exulting in my kill. And that prize I carried home
So proudly was a curse on my own head. Any honor I have
Left can be bestowed only on a dead man,
My son, whose mother's hands,
The hands that slew him, must lay him out decently
For burial—cold comfort for the dead!
Polluted as they are with the curse of my son's blood,
How can I touch his body with these blighted hands ?

KADMOS

Lay hands on him no more—his destruction was
A result of the god's anger. The body is accursed.
Until Bellowing Bromios gives his assent,
What hands in Thebes dare bury it? Its taint
Might spread to all the citizens, who, innocent themselves
Save for their ruler's guilt, may still
Escape pollution, for the full extent of the god's anger
Must, I should think, be satisfied by this boy's death.

AGAUE

O my child, whose hands will then afford you proper care?
Even if your mother's are themselves contaminated,
Can they do greater harm than they have done so far?

As best we can, father, let us try to make
The darling boy whole again, shapely and straight,
So I may fondle his head, kissing
Each and every part of the flesh
That once I bore and brought up with such love.

### KADMOS

Be firm and be assured. Painful an effort though it is,
I will convey Pentheus's bloodied, battered limbs
To a place of decent burial. If this offends the god,
Whatever suffering he sends,
After this loss will seem trifling in comparison,
And at my advanced age cannot last long.

### AGAUE

O gods, what dirge can I intone to crave pardon
Of every broken limb, what lullaby can I croon to lay them
 to rest?
Gathering with loving care these mangled gory limbs,
This flesh I brought into the world, which one shall I mourn
 most?
Why not this hand? Was this the first thing that I seized?
How could I so have ripped my own flesh asunder?
So strong an arm! How flawless was this body!
His feet—so swift and steady in their regal stride!—
Still in their hunting boots. Where is the other? So far so
 good.
And these lifeless genitals, that had no chance
To breed a princely posterity for our house!
Come, Father. We must restore the head to this poor boy.
O fresh and beardless cheek! Sweet boyish mouth!
Now with this veil I shroud your head. And all your
 tortured limbs
And parts I shroud with purple veils, your ribs, shattered
 and bloody.
For the last time, I swaddle him, not as a babe, but as a
 corpse.
Pentheus! My only child! Be at peace!

CHORUS

Let such a scene teach those with eyes to see
Dionysos is the son of Zeus. Any questions?

AGAUE

But why should my son be punished for my mistakes?

KADMOS

He took after you, and would not offer tribute to the god.
And so the god destroyed us all in one fell swoop,
Wiping out the whole family—you and this boy here,
And me, the last surviving male, who must look on
This fruit of your womb, o wretched woman,
Butchered in the nastiest, most disgraceful way;
O child, my flesh-and-blood, you held my dynasty together.
You were the terror of the city; one look at your face
And no one would dare to disrespect this old man,
For you would dole out speedy punishment.
O best beloved of men —for though you are no more
I still count you my best beloved, child—
No more with your hand stroking my chin
And calling me "granddad" will you hug me, child,
Saying, "Who is wronging, who is dishonoring you, old
    man?
"Who is giving you grief, who's pestering you?
"Tell me so I may punish the man who wrongs you,
    granddad."
But now I am steeped in misery, and you are crushed,
Miserable your mother and stricken her sisters.
If there is anyone out there who doubts the gods,
Take a good look at this man's death and be firm in your
faith.

CHORUS

You have all my sympathy, Kadmos; but your grandson
Got what he deserved, however bitter it may be for you.

DIONYSOS

I am that I am—Dionysos is
The son of Zeus, come back to Thebes, revealed

As god to man. I show you my true form, and here above
My mother's tomb, in lightning, just as I was born.

CHORUS
Bellowing Bromios! His voice! Prostrate yourselves!

DIONYSOS
The people of Thebes blasphemed and slandered me,
Declaring I was born of mortal man,
Each and every one; but their ruler outdid them all.
You are my witnesses: Pentheus behaved outrageously;
In his arrogance he tried to bind my hands and imprison me.
Then, mounted on misfortune, he headed for Kithairon
And dared to spy upon my followers in their secret rites.
This man has had the death which he deserved,
Dismembered and dispersed among the jagged rocks.
And he has rightly perished at the hands
Of those who least of all should have caused his death.
What he suffered, he suffered justly.
Now I shall disclose the just sufferings in store for his
    people.
Your city shall be sacked by spear-toting foreigners and
surrendered,
And you will endure many ills, shunted from city to city
As slaves to fellow Greeks.
On you, Agaue, and on your sisters I pronounce this
    sentence
To expiate the murder you committed
You must leave this city, never to set eyes on it again.
You are unclean, and it would be a sacrilege for murderers
To pray unscathed beside the graves of their victims.
Next, I shall disclose the ordeals
That await this man. Kadmos,
You told the truth, but framed it like a lie,
To serve your own self-interest, not your god.
Your hands are far from clean, but since you did not kill,
Three days are allotted to you in which to build
Your grandson a tomb which
Like my mother's, no one must come near.
When you have finished that, you shall not die,
But be turned to a dragon, and your wife,

Harmonia, mortal daughter of the war god Ares,
Shall share your fate, changed to a savage serpent.
And, as the oracle of Zeus decrees, you and your wife
Will drive an ox-cart at the head of troops of barbarians,
And with this monstrous army you shall ravage many
Cities. But after it plunders Apollo's shrine,
It is doomed to return home defeated and disgraced.
Then the god of war will rescue Harmonia and you
And transport you living to the land of those forever blessed.
I speak these things, I, Dionysos, son not of mortal father
But of Zeus; and if you had had the sense to admit that,
The good sense to comply, the seed of Zeus, Dionysos,
Would have been your ally and now you would be happy.

#### KADMOS

Dionysos, we sinned against you. Have pity on us!

#### DIONYSOS

You took your sweet time learning who I am. Your
knowledge comes too late.

#### KADMOS

We realize that now. But your punishments are too severe.

#### DIONYSOS

Yes, because I am a god and you insulted me.

#### KADMOS

Gods should not act from spite like petty mortals!

#### DIONYSOS

Long, long ago my father Zeus assented to these things.

#### AGAUE

Alas, old man, our fate is sealed: cast out of our native land.

#### DIONYSOS

Why do you loiter here when you have no alternative?

KADMOS

O child, to what horrid hardships we have come,
All of us, you, wretched woman, your sisters,
And my unhappy self; I am to live among strangers,
An outsider, an alien old man; and, what is worse, the oracle
 declares
I am ordained to bring to Greece a mongrel army of
 barbarians.
And Ares's child, Harmonia my wife,
And I, changed to dragons, in that horrendous form shall
Direct spear-chuckers to attack Greek tombs and altars,
Nor shall I, wretch that I am, ever be put out of my misery or
Drift down the river of Hades to find peace in death.

AGAUE

O father, I must lose you and go into exile.

KADMOS

Why fling your white arms round me, o hapless child?
Do you think you're a young swan sheltering its old drone
 of a parent,
Hoary and helpless?

AGAUE

I can't help it. But where am I to turn, outcast from my
 hearth and home?

KADMOS

I don't know, child; your father can no longer be of help.

AGAUE

Farewell, o home, farewell o native land and city.
I leave you in desolation,
A displaced person cut off from everything I know and love.

KADMOS

Go now, child, and ask shelter from the son of Aristaios...

AGAUE

I grieve for you, father.

KADMOS

And I for you, child,
And weep sorely for your sisters.

AGAUE

It's monstrous that Lord Dionysos should inflict
This outrage on our house.

DIONYSOS

Because you inflicted monstrous outrages on me,
Dishonoring my name in Thebes.

AGAUE

Farewell, my father.

KADMOS

Farewell, o unhappy
Daughter. You'll have a hard row to hoe before you do fare
  well.

AGAUE

Lead me, o friends, to my sisters
Who will for pity's sake accompany me as fellow-exiles.
Let me go where
Blood-spattered Kithairon cannot look down on me
Nor I lay eyes on Mount Kithairon,
Nor where some joyrod might remind me.
Let such things be matter for other Bakkhai.

CHORUS

Divinity takes a multitude of forms,
And many things that seem unlikely the gods bring to pass;
What seems most likely never does take place;
This time the God brought about what no one could expect.
And that's the way it goes.

END OF PLAY

www.ingramcontent.com/pod-product-compliance
Lightning Source LLC
Chambersburg PA
CBHW052223090426
42741CB00010B/2659